The 13 Keys to Happiness

Unlocking the Secrets to a Joyful Life

Tom Levy

First edition: November 2023

ISBN: 978-2-89864-019-3

Published by: 01 Web Canada

Preface

In this ever-evolving world, where the pursuit of happiness often seems like an elusive quest, "The 13 Keys to Happiness" emerges as a beacon of light. This book is not just a collection of chapters; it is a journey, an exploration into the depths of what truly constitutes a fulfilling and joyful life.

Each chapter of this book unlocks one of the thirteen essential keys to happiness - from the transformative power of gratitude to the serene wisdom of acceptance. As you delve into the pages, you will discover that happiness is not a distant dream, but a tangible reality that can be achieved through conscious practice and mindfulness.

The chapters on physical and mental health emphasize the foundational role of well-being in our pursuit of happiness. They remind us that taking care of our body and mind is not just an act of self-love, but a prerequisite for a joyous life.

In exploring healthy relationships, presence, and connection, this book highlights the significance of our interactions with the world and the people around us. It illustrates how our external connections deeply impact our internal state of happiness.

Passion, resilience, and authenticity are the chapters that encourage you to look within, to find your true self and to courageously follow your heart. They are about embracing your uniqueness and finding strength in your journey.

The chapters on letting go, optimism, balance, and inner wisdom guide you towards a life of harmony and contentment. They teach you to navigate life's ups and downs with grace, to find equilibrium in chaos, and to listen to the quiet, guiding voice within.

As you turn each page, you will find not just words but a mirror reflecting back at you the potential for happiness that resides within you. This book is an invitation, a guide, and a companion on your path to a happier, more balanced, and authentic life.

As you embark on this journey with "The 13 Keys to Happiness," I hope you find within these pages the inspiration, the courage, and the wisdom to unlock the doors to your own joy and contentment.

Welcome to the beginning of your happiest journey.

Table of contents

Introduction

Happiness. A word we often use, yet its meaning seems elusive. Is it a fleeting moment of joy, a passing emotion, or a lasting state of being? Through ages and cultures, happiness has been defined, redefined, celebrated, and pursued with unparalleled zeal. Philosophers, artists, scientists, all have pondered its true nature and the means to achieve it.

For some, happiness is tied to possession, the fulfillment of ambitions, or social recognition. For others, it lies in simple pleasures, human connections, or spiritual realization. But one thing is clear: happiness is essential. It is that force that drives us to rise each morning, to dream, to hope, to connect with each other, and to seek meaning in our existence.

In this book, we will not only explore the ephemeral nature of happiness. We will unveil, step by step, thirteen keys that can open the door to a more authentic, deeper, and lasting happiness. For happiness is not only a fundamental right of every individual, it is also a quest, a journey that we all undertake, consciously or unconsciously, every day of our lives.

Chapter 1: Gratitude

Gratitude is more than just an emotion, an action, or a habit. It's a mindset, a life choice, a lens through which we see the world. Diving deep into gratitude and weaving it into the fabric of our lives might be the most potent key to unlocking happiness.

Grasping Gratitude's Value

Each day throws myriad situations and challenges our way, each with the power to lift us up or knock us down. Amidst this whirlwind, it's easy to fixate on what's awry, what's lacking, or what could be better. But that's where gratitude steps in, urging us to shift our gaze.

Embracing gratitude doesn't mean turning a blind eye to hurdles or glossing over hardships. Instead, it's about acknowledging and cherishing the good in our lives, no matter how big or small. When we opt to view life through gratitude-tinted glasses, moments of happiness, acts of love, and silver linings in the darkest clouds start popping into focus.

The ripple effects of gratitude are manifold:

• **Emotional Well-being:** It acts as an antidote to feelings of envy, bitterness, or regret, paving the way for positive vibes like joy, love, and hope.

• **Physical Health:** Grateful folks often report better heart health, sounder sleep, and a more robust immune response.

• **Resilience:** Gratitude can be our anchor in storms, reminding us of life's genuine treasures.

Daily Doses of Gratitude: Practical Tips

Gratitude Journal: Every evening, spare a few moments to jot down three things that brightened your day. It could be a stranger's smile or something as monumental as a job promotion.

Thank-You Letters: Reflect on someone who's left a positive imprint on your life. Pen down a heartfelt note expressing your gratitude. You could send it or keep it as a cherished memento.

21-Day Gratitude Challenge: For three weeks, pinpoint a fresh reason for your gratitude daily. It'll broaden your horizons, making you an active seeker of joy.

Everyday Reminders: Stick notes bearing messages like "What are you thankful for today?"

on your mirror, computer, or fridge as gentle nudges toward gratitude.

Gratitude Meditation: Carve out a few minutes daily to close your eyes and immerse in the sensations, people, and memories you're most thankful for.

By making these practices a staple in your daily routine, gratitude evolves from an occasional act to a way of life. It becomes a gateway to a treasure trove of happiness, joy, and a profound appreciation for life's wonders, both big and small. Remember, gratitude isn't reserved for the good days; it shines brightest when embraced during the tough times.

Chapitre 2 : Health

Health, a treasure many take for granted, is at the heart of our well-being and fulfillment. It is the pillar that supports every aspect of our life, from the vigor of our days to the depth of our nighttime dreams. By taking care of our body, we provide our mind with a sturdy and tranquil dwelling. In this chapter, we will explore the deep interdependence between physical and mental health, and how they intertwine to influence our perception of happiness and our ability to fully embrace life.

Physical Health

Physical health is not merely the absence of disease or pain; it's a state of complete well-being, a harmony between body and mind. It's the foundation upon which our ability to fully live, to love with fervor, and to chase our dreams with vigor rests.

Symbiosis of Body and Mind

The connection between our body and mind is profound. When our body is in good health, our mind becomes clearer, more alert, and sharper. Conversely, a peaceful and joyous mind promotes better physical health.

Components of Physical Health

Physical health delicately balances various interdependent factors. Among these, nutrition plays a pivotal role. It nourishes, fortifies, and revitalizes our body, all while having a significant impact on our emotional and mental well-being. Consuming nutritious foods, rich in vitamins and minerals, is crucial for our body's optimal function. What we plate up can influence our mood, energy levels, and even our longevity.

Balanced Diet: The Key to Vitality

a. Commonly Consumed Food Perils:

- **Fried Foods:** Though delectable, fried foods can escalate the risk of heart diseases due to their high saturated and trans fat content. Moreover, they contribute to unwanted weight gain.
- **Sodas:** These sugary drinks can not only contribute to weight gain but also heighten the risk of type 2 diabetes and tooth erosion.
- **Sugar:** Overconsumption of sugar can lead to health issues such as obesity, tooth decay, and even heart disorders.
- **Salts:** While salt is essential for health, overconsumption can lead to issues like hypertension and cardiovascular diseases.

b. Optimal Food Choices:

- **Fruits and Vegetables:** Packed with vitamins, minerals, and antioxidants. A variety of these can bolster the immune system and promote radiant skin.
- **Lean Proteins:** Fish, poultry, legumes, and nuts are stellar sources of essential proteins needed for tissue building and repair.
- **Whole Grains:** Foods like quinoa, brown rice, and oats are fiber-rich, promoting healthy digestion and prolonged satiety.
- **Water and Teas:** Adequate hydration is vital for optimal organ function. Teas, especially green tea, can offer antioxidant benefits.

Dietary Supplements (Potential and Caution):

a. Dietary Supplements:

Vitamins and minerals such as Vitamin C, D, zinc, and magnesium can bridge nutritional gaps, especially when obtaining these nutrients solely from food is challenging. However, it's always preferable to consult a health professional before starting any supplement.

b. Herbs and Superfoods:

- **Maca:** Known to boost endurance and libido.
- **Tribulus:** Often used to elevate testosterone levels and enhance muscle performance.
- **Ginger:** Boasts anti-inflammatory properties and is frequently used for digestion.
- **Fenugreek:** Traditionally used to stimulate appetite and support lactation in new mothers.
- **Ginseng:** Celebrated for its revitalizing properties and for boosting energy and concentration.

It's imperative to understand that even if these herbs possess beneficial properties, they must be consumed cautiously, ideally under a professional's supervision, as they might interact with medications or have side effects.

Physical health is a nuanced symphory of deliberate choices and actions. With a balanced diet, a discerning view of supplements and superfoods, and a proactive approach, we can not only strengthen our body but also nourish our spirit.

Regular Physical Activity:

Regular exercise fortifies our heart, enhances blood circulation, and strengthens muscles. But it also plays a pivotal role in releasing endorphins, the happiness hormones.

Physical activity, beyond its benefits for the body, is a vital key to nourishing the spirit and soul. It can be a source of joy, challenge, and accomplishment, providing a unique path to self-discovery. To harness the full benefits of physical activity, it's vital to pick a sport or exercise that resonates personally, something that becomes a passion rather than a chore.

- **Team Sports:** These encompass games like soccer, basketball, volleyball, and rugby. Such sports cultivate team spirit, reinforce social bonds, and teach essential values like cooperation and communication. Playing in a team motivates each member, making the experience more engaging.
- **Individual Sports:** These include activities like running, cycling, and tennis. They offer a chance to focus on personal goals, challenge boundaries, and learn discipline and determination.
- **Combat Sports:** Boxing, judo, karate, and jiu-jitsu, among others, not only enhance

physical strength and stamina but also self-control, respect, and focus.

- **Swimming:** Swimming is a low-impact activity that strengthens the entire body. It's also therapeutic, offering a moment of relaxation and moving meditation.
- **Yoga:** More than just exercise, yoga is a practice that unifies body, mind, and soul. It enhances flexibility, strength, and balance while fostering relaxation and mindfulness.
- **Endurance Sports:** Marathons, triathlons, and other endurance races push individuals beyond their limits, fostering perseverance and resilience.
- **Recreational Activities:** Dancing, hiking, gardening, or even daily walks can be equally beneficial. These activities can often be incorporated into daily routines without feeling like structured "exercise".

It's essential to remember that the best exercise is the one you love and continue doing. Physical activity shouldn't be perceived as a chore but as an opportunity to engage, disconnect, have fun, and ultimately, celebrate what our body can achieve. Find your passion and let that enthusiasm guide your journey towards enhanced physical and mental health.

The Essence of Quality Sleep

Restorative sleep is essential for the recovery and regeneration of our body. It enhances our concentration, boosts our immune system, and prepares us for a new day. Sleep is not merely a break in our daily routine; it is a fundamental necessity that affects every aspect of our well-being. It is as vital as the air we breathe, the water we drink, and the food we eat. Let's delve into a deep understanding of the significance of quality sleep.

- **Repair and Regeneration:** While we sleep, our body actively works to repair muscles, synthesize proteins, and renew cells. Damaged tissues are mended, thus promoting better physical health.
- **Memory Consolidation:** Sleep plays a pivotal role in processing and consolidating the day's memories. During REM sleep, our brain sorts, stores, and solidifies what we learned during the day.
- **Hormonal Regulation:** Numerous hormonal processes, like insulin regulation, growth hormone release, and cortisol production, mainly occur during sleep. Proper sleep ensures these hormonal processes function optimally.
- **Emotional Balance:** The quality of our sleep directly influences our mood and

emotional stability. Disrupted sleep can lead to feelings of irritability, depression, or anxiety.

- **Strengthening the Immune System:** Adequate sleep boosts our natural defense against infections, allowing our immune system to function at its peak.
- **Enhancement of Concentration and Productivity:** Sound sleep sharpens attention, enhances concentration, and fuels creativity, making us more efficient and productive in our daily tasks.
- **Disease Prevention**: Chronic lack of sleep is linked to an increased risk of conditions like obesity, diabetes, cardiovascular diseases, and even certain types of cancer.

To ensure quality sleep, it's crucial to maintain a regular routine, create a sleep-conducive environment (darkness, quiet, appropriate temperature), avoid screens before sleeping, and watch one's diet. For instance, caffeine is a stimulant that can disrupt your sleep if consumed late in the day.

Practices to Improve Sleep Quality

For many of us, even recognizing the importance of sleep, falling and staying asleep can be a significant challenge. Here are some practices and tips that can help improve sleep quality:

- **Sleep Hygiene:** Maintain a regular routine. Try to go to bed and wake up at the same time every day, even on weekends. This consistency reinforces your body's internal clock and improves the quality of your nighttime sleep.
- **Bedroom Ambiance:** Ensure your bedroom is conducive to sleep. This means a dark, quiet, and cool room. Consider using eye masks, earplugs, humidifiers, fans, and white noise machines to create an optimal environment.
- **Limit Screen Exposure:** The blue light emitted by phones, tablets, computers, and TVs inhibits melatonin production, the hormone controlling your sleep-wake cycle. Try to disconnect at least an hour before bedtime.
- **Avoid Heavy Meals Before Bed:** Heavy meals can cause indigestion that interferes with sleep. If you're hungry right before bedtime, opt for a light snack.
- **Physical Activity:** Regular exercise can help you fall asleep faster and enjoy deeper sleep. However, don't exercise too close to bedtime, as it might have the opposite effect.
- **Relaxation Techniques:** Methods like meditation, deep breathing, and

visualization can help calm the mind and prepare the body for sleep. Consider these techniques as a way to "unwind" from the day's pressure.

- **Limit Daytime Naps:** If you're in the habit of napping, try limiting it to 20-30 minutes and avoid sleeping in the afternoon.
- **Avoid Alcohol, Caffeine, and Sugary Drinks:** These substances can disrupt your sleep. Try to limit your intake, especially later in the day.
- **Sleep-promoting Plants and Supplements:** Several plants and supplements are known for their ability to promote relaxation and enhance sleep. For instance, chamomile is often consumed as tea for its calming properties. Valerian is another plant that, when used as a supplement, can help reduce the time it takes to fall asleep. Magnesium plays a role in sleep regulation, and its supplementation might benefit those struggling to stay asleep. Lastly, melatonin, a hormone naturally produced by the body, is also available as a supplement and is widely used to regulate sleep cycles, especially to counteract the effects of jet lag. However, it's crucial to consult a health professional before introducing new supplements to your

routine, ensuring they are suitable for your needs and that there are no contraindications.

- **Consult a Professional:** If, despite all your efforts, you continue to struggle with sleep or feel excessively drowsy during the day, it might be beneficial to consult a doctor or sleep specialist.

In the end, it's essential to view sleep as a priority, not an option. It might require adjustments or experimenting with different strategies to find what works best for you, but every positive step you take towards improving your sleep is an investment in your overall well-being.

Physical Health as the Key to Happiness

Having a healthy body grants us the freedom to explore, discover, and love unconditionally. It allows us to dance in the rain, climb mountains, and chase our passions without being held back by pain or fatigue.

Habits to Maintain Robust Physical Health

- **Exercise Routine:** Be it walking, yoga, swimming, or any other sport, find what you love and incorporate it into your daily routine.

- **Hydration:** Drink sufficient water each day to keep your body hydrated and help flush out toxins.
- **Avoid Unhealthy Foods:** Fried foods, sodas, etc.
- **Avoid Excess:** Whether it's alcohol, caffeine, sugar, or salt, moderation is key.

Prioritize Quality Sleep: Ensure you get restorative sleep each night.

Meditations and Relaxation Techniques: While they might seem focused on the mind, they have a profound impact on physical health by reducing stress and promoting relaxation.

By prioritizing excellent physical health, you're not just betting on your present well-being but also laying the foundation for a life filled with dynamism, joy, and fulfillment. Always remember that your body is unique and irreplaceable; honor it, cherish it, and in return, it will reward you with unparalleled vitality.

Mental Health

Mental health, just like physical health, is a crucial element of our well-being. It encompasses our emotional, psychological, and social balance. It affects how we think, feel, and act in various life situations. It plays a pivotal role in our ability to handle stress, relate to others, and make decisions.

The Complexity of the Mind

The human mind is a complex wonder, capable of creating, dreaming, and experiencing a spectrum of emotions ranging from exuberant joy to deep sadness. However, just like the body, the mind can also suffer and need care.

The True Essence of Mental Health

Emotional balance: The ability to experience emotions, whether positive or negative, without being overwhelmed by them.

Resilience: The inner strength that allows us to bounce back from life's adversities and challenges.

Self-esteem: A positive and realistic perception of oneself, recognizing both our strengths and weaknesses.

Pillars of Mental Health:

Medication and Its Role

It's essential to acknowledge that, for some, medication can play a vital role in managing and treating mental disorders. Antidepressants, anxiolytics, and other drugs can offer much-needed relief for many, allowing them to lead a balanced life. However, it's crucial to consult a healthcare professional to discuss the benefits and risks associated with medication.

Dietary Supplements and Mental Well-being

Certain dietary supplements, like magnesium, zinc, omega-3s, and others, are known for their ability to support mental health. Plants like St. John's wort are also used as natural remedies for mild to moderate depression.

The Impact of Mental Health on Happiness

A healthy mind can see beauty in the everyday, find hope in adversity, and create meaning even in the darkest moments. It provides us with clarity to understand ourselves and the world around us while giving us the freedom to choose our ath to happiness.

Strategies to Nourish the Mind

- **Therapy and Counseling:** A safe space to explore and understand one's feelings, emotions, and behaviors.
- **Meditation and Mindfulness:** Cultivating presence and awareness to create inner peace.
- **Journaling:** A way to express, reflect on, and break down one's thoughts.
- **Social Connection:** Nurturing deep and meaningful relationships that offer support and understanding.

Plants to Enhance Mood and Well-being

Several plants are known for their antidepressant virtues or for improving mood and mental well-being. It's essential to note that the effectiveness of these plants can vary among individuals, and their use should always be supervised by a healthcare professional, especially if you're already on medication or have specific health conditions. Some often mentioned plants for their mood-enhancing properties include:

1. **St. John's wort (Hypericum perforatum):** Probably one of the best-known plants for its antidepressant effects. Numerous studies suggest it might be as

effective as some conventional antidepressants for treating mild to moderate depression.

2. **Rhodiola (Rhodiola rosea):** An adaptogenic plant used for centuries in Europe and Asia to increase resistance to physical and emotional stress. It's often recommended for combating fatigue, improving concentration, and supporting mood.

3. **Griffonia simplicifolia:** A natural source of 5-HTP (5-hydroxytryptophan), a precursor to serotonin, a neurotransmitter involved in mood regulation. 5-HTP is often used as a dietary supplement to improve mood and fight depression.

4. **Chamomile (Matricaria recutita):** Although mostly known for its relaxing and sedative properties, some studies suggest chamomile might also have antidepressant effects.

5. **Valerian (Valeriana officinalis):** Traditionally used to treat insomnia and anxiety, it might indirectly help improve mood by enhancing sleep quality.

6. **Saffron (Crocus sativus):** Studies have shown saffron might have antidepressant effects comparable to some commonly prescribed antidepressant drugs.

7. **Holy Basil (Ocimum sanctum):** Also known as "Tulsi", it's often used in Ayurvedic medicine to treat stress, anxiety, and depression.
8. **Passionflower (Passiflora incarnata):** Traditionally used to treat anxiety, insomnia, and nervousness, it might also positively affect mood.

It's crucial to remember that while these plants can offer support in managing mood disorders, they don't replace comprehensive medical treatment. If you or someone you know suffers from depression or other mood disorders, it's imperative to consult a healthcare professional.

Limiting Media Overconsumption

Too much information, especially when negative, can overwhelm the mind. Taking regular breaks from media and focusing on the present can help maintain mental balance.

Protecting and nourishing our mental health is an ongoing journey, not a final destination. It's a commitment to oneself, an act of self-love. By prioritizing our mental well-being, we open the door to a richer, more fulfilling, and ultimately happier life.

Conclusion

Mental health, often a complex and deeply personal journey, is an integral part of our overall well-being. It's a path marked by ups and downs, challenges and triumphs, and it requires not only our attention but also our compassion and understanding. In this journey, it's crucial to recognize that reaching out for help is not a sign of weakness, but rather a courageous step towards self-care and healing. Seeking assistance, whether it's through therapy, medication, or leaning on a support system of friends and family, is an act of bravery and strength. It's about acknowledging that we don't have to navigate the complexities of our minds alone. Therapy offers a safe space to explore our thoughts and emotions, to understand the root causes of our struggles, and to develop strategies for coping and growth. Medication, when needed, can be a vital tool in balancing the chemical aspects of our mental health, bringing stability and clarity. Meanwhile, social support provides the invaluable reassurance that we are not isolated in our experiences. It's a reminder that others care, understand, and are willing to stand by us. Embracing these forms of help is a testament to an individual's resilience and commitment to their mental health journey. It's about taking control of one's life and making choices that foster well-being and inner peace.

Chapter 3: Healthy Relationships

The relationships we maintain largely dictate the quality of our lives. They act as reflections of our emotions and catalysts for personal growth. Within this delicate balance of connecting with others while preserving oneself, it's crucial to understand the significance of fostering healthy bonds while reserving a sacred space for oneself. This chapter will guide you through the art of building rewarding relationships while setting boundaries that respect and safeguard your personal and emotional space.

Social Connection and Healthy Relationships

The relationships we foster play a pivotal role in our overall well-being and happiness. Being surrounded by individuals who support, value, and understand us is paramount to our personal growth.

Choosing Your Relationships: Understand that the quality of relationships greatly outweighs quantity. Surround yourself with individuals who uplift you, inspire you, and push you to become the best version of yourself.

Avoiding Toxic People: Toxicity can sap our energy, dent our self-worth, and even alter our life outlook. While challenging, it's paramount to identify and distance oneself from toxic relationships. When these individuals are close relatives or family, it becomes trickier. In such instances, it's advised to set clear boundaries, voice your feelings openly, and if necessary, seek professional guidance. The goal isn't necessarily severing ties but preserving your well-being by establishing healthy boundaries.

Setting Boundaries: It's imperative to set clear boundaries in our interactions to ensure mutual respect. Boundaries help protect us and maintain a healthy relationship with ourselves and others.

Nurturing Deep Relationships: Aim to cultivate relationships that provide genuine meaning, profound connection, and mutual understanding.

Self-Preservation

Being empathetic creatures, we often find ourselves drawn to the emotions and experiences of others, bearing a deep-seated desire to assist, support, and alleviate. However, it's vital to recognize that our ability to aid others hinges directly on our own well-being. Self-preservation isn't an act of selfishness but rather an act of self-love that, in turn, lets us love and assist others more effectively.

The Weight of Others' Emotions

While it's natural to want to provide solace when a loved one is in distress, it's also vital to recognize the limits of our capacity. Taking on the woes and emotions of others can overwhelm, tire, and mentally and emotionally exhaust us.

The Significance of Self-Preservation

Establishing Boundaries: Learning to say "no" or to step back isn't a sign of weakness or insensitivity. It's an acknowledgment that to assist effectively, we need to first be at peace and healthy ourselves.

Self-compassion: Treat yourself with the kindness and understanding you'd extend to a friend. Recognizing that you can't solve everything for everyone is vital for your well-being.

Emotional Detachment: This doesn't mean becoming indifferent but maintaining a certain emotional distance to prevent being swamped by others' emotions.

Tools for Self-Preservation

Mindfulness Practices: Learning to remain grounded in the present can assist in recognizing and managing overwhelming emotions.

Journaling: Writing out your feelings can offer perspective and a means to understand and process your emotions.

Therapy: A therapist can equip you with tools and strategies to manage stress, anxiety, and other emotions stemming from dealing with others' issues.

Me-time: Whether it's a solitary walk, some reading time, or just a quick nap, grant yourself moments to rejuvenate.

Self-preservation is a balancing act between opening up to others and shielding one's own mind and heart. By acknowledging your needs and instituting strategies to cater to them, you're not just setting yourself up for lasting personal happiness and health, but also positioning yourself to be a beacon of strength and support for those around you.

Chapter 4: Presence

Living in a world that's always in motion can easily make us lose sight of the significance of the present moment. We often find ourselves caught up in the shadows of past regrets or the anxieties of the future, neglecting the "now". However, the true secret to happiness lies in our ability to be fully in the moment.

The Significance of Living in the Now

To live in the now means to be alert and cherish each moment as it unfolds, without judgment or comparison to another time. It's about wholly immersing oneself in the current experience, whether it's pleasant or challenging.

Breaking Free from the Past

Each of us carries memories, regrets, or past decisions that have left an impression. But instead of seeing these moments as scars, we can view them as badges of honor, testaments to our resilience and our ability to rise above challenges. Every trial, every misstep, and every pain we've experienced has taught us a lesson. These painful times can be seen as teachers, guiding us towards a deeper understanding of ourselves and the world around us. They shape our character, bolster our resolve, and prepare us for future challenges.

Holding onto the past can become a needless burden. The past is set in stone. It's crucial to realize that constantly replaying these moments in our minds doesn't alter reality and can hold us back. By shifting our perspective on our past and seeing each experience as a learning opportunity, we pave the way for healing, growth, and progress. Accepting our past experiences, good or bad, is essential for inner peace and paves the way for a brighter future.

Letting Go of Future Worries

The future is a realm of unknowns. It's a blank canvas with no paint on it yet. However, this doesn't mean we shouldn't prepare or make wise choices for our future. In fact, living in the present means recognizing and maximizing what we can control today. Every action, every decision we make today, is a step toward building our future. The key is to act with the best intentions and information we currently have, without being paralyzed by fear of the unknown.

Too often, we waste our energy fretting over scenarios that may never come to pass. Such worries can stifle our actions and harm our well-being. Instead, by embracing the present moment, we are better equipped to make informed decisions that can positively impact our future.

Embrace uncertainty as an inevitable part of life and remember that even though we can't predict every aspect of our future, we have the power to influence its course by acting mindfully and purposefully today. Focus on what's currently within your grasp, do your best with the knowledge and resources you have, and seek opportunities in the "now". By doing so, you're not only building a promising future but also living a full and meaningful life each day.

The Power of Mindfulness

Practicing mindfulness means training ourselves to focus on the present moment. It's a way to deeply connect with our senses, avoid distraction, and feel profound peace. Meditation, journaling, or simply taking moments to breathe deeply can aid in cultivating this state of mind.

In the end, life is a series of present moments. By choosing to fully live each one, we choose a richer, more meaningful, and ultimately happier life. Here's why it's crucial:

• **Peacefulness:** By concentrating on the now, we diminish distractions and mental turbulence, leading to greater inner peace.

• **Enhanced Appreciation:** Being present allows us to notice and appreciate life's details and nuances that we might otherwise overlook.

• **Stress Reduction:** Dwelling on the past or fretting over the future are significant stress sources. By living in the present, we free our minds from these burdens.

Mindfulness and Meditation Techniques

Mindful Breathing: Take a few minutes daily to focus solely on your breathing. Feel the air going in and out of your lungs. It's a simple method to anchor your mind to the present.

Meditative Walks: As you walk, whether to work or just for a stroll, be mindful of each step. Feel your feet hitting the ground and observe your surroundings without judgment.

Sitting Meditation: Sit comfortably, close your eyes, and concentrate on your breath or a mantra. When your mind drifts, gently bring it back to center. Today, numerous mobile apps can guide and facilitate meditation, offering sessions suitable for all skill levels.

Body Scan: Lie down and focus on every part of your body, starting from your toes and moving up to your head. Notice every sensation without judgment.

Active Listening Practice: Truly listen when speaking to someone. Be fully present in the conversation without thinking about your next response.

Mindful Eating: Be aware of every bite as you eat. Relish the flavors, textures, and aromas of each piece.

Scientific Evidence

Various studies vouch for the benefits of mindfulness and meditation. For instance:

Emotional Well-being: A study in the "Journal of Clinical Psychology" found that mindfulness-based meditation can effectively reduce symptoms of stress, anxiety, and depression.

Physical Health: A systematic review in the "Journal of Psychosomatic Research" discovered that meditation might have beneficial effects on several physiological conditions, including blood pressure, heart diseases, and chronic pain.

Focus: Researchers from the University of Wisconsin-Madison found that meditation training positively impacts sustained attention.

Creativity: A study in "Frontiers in Cognition" examined meditation's effects on creativity and found that certain meditation forms can enhance divergent thinking, a critical creativity indicator.

Thus, these studies back the idea that mindfulness and meditation have numerous benefits, emotionally and physically, and can enhance focus and creativity.

Mindfulness and meditation are powerful tools that can guide us to dwell more deeply in the present moment. With practice, these techniques can not only boost our emotional well-being but also our physical health, focus, and creativity. Perhaps, the key to happiness lies less in the events we experience and more in how we choose to experience them.

Chapter 5 : Acceptance

One of the greatest sources of suffering in human life stems from our resistance to change, the unknown, and the unexpected. Yet, the ebb and flow of tides, changing seasons, birth, and death are all integral parts of life. If we can learn to gracefully accept these inevitable changes, we can find lasting happiness.

Accepting what we cannot change

Life doesn't always unfold as we planned. Unexpected events, tragedies, failures, and disappointments happen. In these situations, we often feel that life is unfair. However, fighting these realities only amplifies our suffering.

Accepting that life isn't always fair is a crucial step towards inner peace. Expecting every situation to be balanced or for every person to treat us with fairness and acknowledgment is a recipe for disillusionment. Each individual has their own perception of justice, influenced by their experiences, culture, and beliefs. Instead of constantly seeking external fairness, let's focus on our own integrity and how we react to life's twists and turns. Finding balance within ourselves and acting kindly, regardless of the world's response, is a far more sustainable source of contentment.

Recognition of reality: Before we can accept a situation, we first need to recognize and admit it. This doesn't mean we have to like what's happening, but simply acknowledge the reality of the situation.

Letting go of "if onlys": Dwelling on what could have been only adds to our pain. Letting go of regrets and "if only" scenarios is essential to move forward.

Finding serenity: Often, by accepting what we can't change, we find inner peace. As the famous Serenity Prayer goes: "Grant me the serenity to accept the things I cannot change, the courage to change the things I can, and the wisdom to know the difference."

The difference between resignation and acceptance

Resignation and acceptance may seem similar at first glance, but they are fundamentally different in their nature and implications.

Resignation: Resignation is a feeling of defeatism. It's the sense of being beaten, of giving up, and yielding to the situation. It's a passive attitude where one feels there's nothing else to do but submit to reality.

Acceptance: Acceptance, on the other hand, is active and involves awareness. It requires a deep understanding of the situation and a conscious choice to embrace that reality while acknowledging that it doesn't define our worth or potential.

By accepting, we take power over the situation. We choose not to be defined or limited by it. Instead, we look beyond the current circumstances to new possibilities and opportunities.

Conclusion

Acceptance doesn't mean resigning to fate or feeling powerless. It's rather a conscious choice to embrace reality, recognize its limitations, and focus on the things we can indeed change. By cultivating acceptance in our lives, we can find enduring inner peace and greater resilience against life's challenges.

Chapter 6: Connection

At the heart of the human experience lies the innate desire for connection. Whether it's with family, friends, partners, or strangers, the ability to connect with others often gives profound meaning to our existence. It's no coincidence that when asking elderly people what they cherish the most, the answer often revolves around the relationships they've nurtured over the years.

The importance of human relationships

Emotional well-being: Healthy relationships offer support, love, and a sense of belonging. They can combat loneliness and provide comfort in challenging times.

Personal growth: Through our interactions with others, we learn about ourselves, face challenges, and grow. Relationships act as a mirror, reflecting our strengths and weaknesses.

Physical health: Strong relationships have been proven to boost physical health. Loneliness or isolation can have negative impacts, increasing the risk of illnesses.

Longevity: Surprisingly, studies have shown that strong relationships can even increase one's lifespan. Human connection nourishes us at a cellular level.

Tips for establishing and maintaining strong connections

Active listening: Pay attention to the words and emotions of the other person. Listen to understand, not necessarily to reply.

Honesty and transparency: Be authentic in your relationships. Trust is the foundation of any strong bond.

Invest time: Relationships require time and effort. Schedule regular times to connect with loved ones, whether it's for a quick call or a quiet dinner.

Set boundaries: Not all connections are beneficial. It's essential to recognize when a relationship is toxic and establish boundaries to protect your well-being.

Celebrate together: Share the good times and support each other during challenging periods. Shared joy is doubled, and shared sorrow is halved.

Develop empathy: Put yourself in the other person's shoes and try to see the world from their perspective. Empathy strengthens mutual understanding.

Conclusion

Beyond individual achievements and material possessions, it's the relationships we cultivate that add color, depth, and meaning to our lives. In an increasingly digitized world, it's imperative to cherish these human connections and constantly work to strengthen them. Because, in the end, connection is what ties everything together in the intricate dance of life.

Chapter 7: Passion

Ah, passion! It is often described as the fire that burns within us, the engine that drives us to excel, the breath that adds color to our most monotonous days. But what exactly is passion? And how can it play an essential role in our quest for happiness?

Finding and pursuing your passion

Self-reflection: First and foremost, it's crucial to understand what excites you. Take the time to think about your interests, what you enjoy doing when no one is watching, and what makes your heart beat a little faster.

Try new things: Sometimes, we don't know what we're passionate about until we discover it. Don't hesitate to step out of your comfort zone and explore new activities or hobbies.

Listen to your emotions: Your body and emotions can give you clues about what truly ignites your passion. If an activity brings joy, excitement, or even a kind of thrilling fear, it might be a budding passion.

Commit: Once you've identified a passion, fully commit to it. This doesn't necessarily mean you have to turn it into a career, but give it some priority and time in your life.

How passion influences happiness

Purpose and direction: Having a passion gives life meaning. It provides direction, a goal, something to look forward to.

Personal fulfillment: Pursuing passion fosters personal growth. By tackling challenges and learning new things, you feel accomplished and proud.

Stress reduction: Immersing yourself in an activity you love can act as a form of meditation. It offers an escape, a moment where life's worries can be set aside.

Connecting with others: Passions often have a social component. Whether by joining a club, taking classes, or simply sharing your passion with others, it can lead to meaningful connections.

Vitality and energy: Passion can act as fuel, giving you the energy and motivation needed to face the day with enthusiasm.

Scientific studies:

A study from Yale University and Oxford University found that individuals passionate about their work and daily activities tend to live longer and have better mental health.

Research from the University of South Carolina discovered that people who regularly pursue their passions have better engagement levels, are more satisfied with their lives, and have higher self-esteem.

Testimonies from famous individuals:

Steve Jobs frequently spoke about the importance of following one's passion. In his renowned speech at Stanford University, he said, "The only way to do great work is to love what you do. If you haven't found it yet, keep looking. Don't settle."

Oprah Winfrey, one of the world's most influential figures, often stressed the importance of passion for success. She stated, "Passion is energy. Feel the power that comes from focusing on what excites you."

Nelson Mandela remarked, "There is no passion in playing small, in settling for a life that is less than the one you are capable of living."

Conclusion

Passion isn't just a mere distraction or a hobby. It's a profound source of joy, fulfillment, and growth. By finding and nurturing this inner fire, we not only enrich our own lives but also bring light to those around us. In our pursuit of happiness, recognizing, embracing, and following our passions is a vital step.

Chapter 8: Resilience

Life, in its beauty and complexity, is dotted with highs and lows. Each one of us, at one point or another, faces challenges that test our strength, patience, and faith. This is where resilience comes into play, this incredible ability to bounce back after trials, overcome adversities, and transform challenges into opportunities for growth.

Here are tangible examples of well-known personalities who demonstrated remarkable resilience in the face of adversity:

Stephen Hawking: Despite being diagnosed with a degenerative disease at the age of 21, which progressively paralyzed him and confined him to a wheelchair, Hawking never let his condition stop him from pursuing his passions. He became one of the most renowned physicists of our time and significantly contributed to our understanding of the universe.

Malala Yousafzai: At the age of 15, she was targeted for assassination by the Taliban because of her advocacy for girls' education in Pakistan. She survived and became a global advocate for women's rights and education, receiving the Nobel Peace Prize at the age of 17.

Nelson Mandela: After spending 27 years in prison for his efforts to end apartheid in South Africa, Mandela was released and became the country's first black president. Instead of seeking revenge, he advocated for reconciliation and worked to unite a divided nation.

Frida Kahlo: After suffering a severe bus accident at the age of 18, Kahlo lived a life of constant physical pain. However, she used her suffering as inspiration for her artworks, becoming one of the most iconic artists in history.

These examples demonstrate the human ability to persevere in the face of obstacles, to turn tragedies into triumphs, and to find hope even in the darkest moments. These stories of resilience can inspire anyone going through challenging times.

But how does one develop this essential skill? Let's dive into the world of resilience.

Overcoming Adversities

Recognition of Reality: Accepting the reality is the first step in overcoming any adversity. It doesn't mean you have to be happy or content with the situation, but merely recognize what is.

Look for the Positive: Even in the toughest situations, there can be a positive aspect or a lesson to be learned. It could be as simple as learning something new about yourself or strengthening valuable relationships.

Avoid Comparison: Every individual faces different adversities. Comparing your pain to others' can minimize your feelings. It's crucial to understand that every experience is valid and unique.

Seek Support: Surrounding yourself with caring and understanding people can make all the difference. Talking about your feelings and sharing your experiences can help you process and heal.

Techniques to Develop Resilience

Take Care of Your Physical Health: A healthy body can better handle stress. This includes a balanced diet, regular exercise, and adequate sleep.

Establish Routines: Having a daily routine can provide a sense of normality. It can also be a reminder of things you control when everything seems out of control.

Set Achievable Goals: Give yourself clear and achievable goals to help you move forward. It can provide a sense of purpose and direction.

Adopt a Growth Mindset: Believe that you have the ability to grow and evolve through your experiences. Every challenge is an opportunity for growth.

Practice Meditation and Mindfulness: These techniques can help keep your mind centered, reduce stress, and improve concentration.

Journaling: Keeping a journal can help clarify your thoughts, process your emotions, and track your progress over time.

Conclusion

Resilience isn't innate; it's a skill that can be developed and strengthened over time and with practice. By nurturing this inner strength, we not only prepare ourselves to face life's storms but also come out stronger, wiser, and more fulfilled. Resilience, at the heart of the pursuit of happiness, is that spark that drives us to keep going, even in the face of obstacles.

Chapter 9: Authenticity

In a world where the pressure to conform is ever-present, staying true to oneself can be challenging. Yet, authenticity is one of the most valuable keys to happiness. It allows us to lead enriching, honest, and meaningful lives. Let's delve deeper into this essential virtue.

Being authentic doesn't mean expressing everything we think or feel without a filter. It means recognizing and accepting our values, beliefs, flaws, and strengths. However, this authenticity should be exercised with responsibility and discernment.

For instance, if someone harbors biases or discriminatory ideas, being authentic doesn't grant carte blanche to spread or act on them. Instead, authenticity in this context should lead to introspection, questioning why one feels this way and actively working to overcome such biases. Authenticity also paves the way for personal growth.

Thus, authenticity isn't a justification for ignorance or harm. On the contrary, it should urge us to be better, to seek understanding and empathy, and to align our actions with positive values. In the pursuit of personal truth, we must also ensure that our truths don't hinder the happiness or well-being of others.

Ultimately, authenticity is a quest for balance between staying true to oneself while being aware of and respectful to the world around us. It's in this balance that true happiness can be found.

Being True to Oneself:

Self-awareness: The first step to being authentic is to know oneself. This means being aware of one's values, beliefs, desires, emotions, and motivations.

Authenticity with respect for others: Although society might sometimes push us to adopt behaviors or attitudes that aren't entirely true to ourselves, being authentic doesn't mean giving free rein to every impulse or thought. It's about living true to our values while respecting others and considering the context in which we operate.

Self-compassion: Accepting who we are, including our weaknesses, is crucial for authenticity. This requires self-compassion and kindness.

The Importance of Honesty and Integrity:

The pillars of authenticity: Honesty and integrity are fundamental for living an authentic life. They compel us to act in line with our beliefs and to stay true to ourselves in all situations.

Self-respect: When we are honest and have integrity, we gain a profound respect for ourselves. This boosts our self-esteem and confidence.

Building strong relationships: Authenticity is essential for establishing and maintaining healthy relationships. When we are genuine and transparent, it inspires trust and respect in others.

Mental and emotional well-being: Being inauthentic can lead to stress, anxiety, and other emotional issues. Conversely, living authentically frees us from these burdens and promotes mental well-being.

Conclusion :

Authenticity is more than just a buzzword. It's a commitment to oneself, a lifestyle that demands courage, awareness, and compassion. By choosing to be authentic, we opt to lead lives filled with meaning, happiness, and truth. In a world of facades, being oneself might be the most precious gift we can give, to both ourselves and others.

Chapter 10 : Letting Go

In a world where we are constantly urged to do more, achieve more, and be more, the act of letting go might seem counterproductive. Yet, paradoxically, it is by loosening our grip on certain things that we find true balance and profound tranquility. This chapter delves into the intricate dance of detachment and how it can pave the way for genuine happiness.

Sophie, a senior executive in a prominent firm, shares, "I was fixated on achieving perfection at work. The fear of failure loomed large, and I wore myself out trying to control everything. It took a burnout for me to grasp the significance of letting go. I've since learned to delegate, accept that I can't control everything, and to live in the now. This not only bolstered me professionally but personally too."

Max's story is equally telling. Following a heart-wrenching breakup, he spent years dwelling on the past and reproaching himself for mistakes made. A chance meeting with a life coach enlightened him about the merit of letting go. "I realized clinging to my past only intensified my pain. By learning to let go, I was able to heal and move forward."

These accounts, and many more, underscore how vital letting go is for our well-being and happiness. It's a skill we can all cultivate with patience and practice.

The Significance of Releasing What No Longer Serves Us:

The Weight of the Past: Clinging to regrets, past mistakes, or grievances can be draining. Letting go creates room for the present and future possibilities.

Emotional Unburdening: Be it anger, envy, or sorrow, holding onto negative emotions harms our mental health and hinders us from fully experiencing the present.

Welcoming New Horizons: By shedding beliefs, attitudes, or behaviors that no longer benefit us, we open the door to fresh perspectives and opportunities.

Techniques for Practicing Detachment:

Meditation: Meditation offers us a vantage point to view our thoughts and emotions. It provides a space to observe without judgment and to release what's unneeded.

Journaling: Regular writing can aid in pinpointing what we're holding onto and why. Once identified, these patterns or beliefs can be more easily released.

Acceptance: To truly let go, we first need to accept reality as it is. This doesn't mean we have to agree, but rather to recognize and accept what exists.

Practice Non-Judgment: By refraining from judging situations and people (including ourselves), we lessen our emotional attachment and can approach matters with clearer vision.

Surround Yourself with Positivity: Individuals and environments that champion our journey towards detachment are invaluable allies. Seek out support groups, mentors, or friends who understand and champion the art of letting go.

Conclusion:

Letting go, often misconceived as a form of surrender or passivity, is in reality a skill of profound empowerment and active choice. It is a practice that we can refine over time, through conscious effort and introspection. Far from being about giving up, letting go is about making intentional choices regarding what we allow to occupy our minds and lives. It involves a deep understanding of our values, desires, and limitations, and the courage to release what no longer serves us or aligns with our goals. This process is not always easy, as it often means parting with familiar habits, thoughts, or even relationships that we have outgrown. Yet, in this act of release, we find an unparalleled form of freedom and peace. By letting go of past grievances, outdated beliefs, and unproductive worries, we open ourselves to new possibilities and a lighter way of being. It allows us to prioritize our well-being and happiness, focusing our energy and attention on what truly uplifts and fulfills us. Through this practice, we learn to live more in the present, appreciate the now, and cultivate a sense of tranquility and contentment in our lives. Letting go becomes a transformative process, a journey of self-discovery and liberation, leading us to a more balanced, joyful, and meaningful existence.

Chapter 11: Optimism

In a world where negative news seems to perpetually dominate the headlines and personal challenges can occasionally feel overwhelming, cultivating optimism might seem like a challenge in itself. However, embracing a positive outlook is not merely a way to uplift one's spirits but is also a potent catalyst for change, resilience, and well-being. In this chapter, we'll dive deep into the art of optimism and how it can transform every aspect of our lives.

Embracing a Positive Outlook:

The Power of Focus: Our mind naturally gravitates toward what it concentrates on. By steering our focus towards the positive, we innately nurture a more optimistic outlook.

Reframing Challenges: Instead of perceiving hurdles as insurmountable barriers, view them as opportunities for learning or growth.

Celebrating Small Wins: It's vital to recognize and celebrate even minor achievements. This solidifies our belief that progress is attainable, and the best is yet to come.

Surround Yourself with Optimistic People: Energy is contagious. Spending time with individuals who see the glass as half full can aid us in adopting a similar perspective.

The Health Impact of Optimism:

Stress Reduction: Optimists typically handle stress more effectively, viewing stressful situations as temporary and conquerable.

Boosted Immune System: Studies have shown that optimistic individuals tend to fall sick less frequently and recover more swiftly when they do.

Enhanced Heart Health: Optimism correlates with lower blood pressure, better heart health, and a reduced risk of heart diseases.

Increased Longevity: Multiple studies have indicated that optimistic individuals tend to live longer than their pessimistic counterparts.

Mental Well-being: Optimism is closely associated with a lower prevalence of depression and an overall enhanced quality of life.

Conclusion:

Optimism isn't just a state of mind; it's also a conscious choice we make daily. By electing to see the brighter side of things, not only do we elevate our mood and perspective, but we also reap a plethora of health and well-being benefits. Adopting a positive outlook is a pivotal step on the journey to lasting happiness.

Chapter 12: Balance

Balance, that harmonious point between extremes, is a fundamental key to happiness. It is often spoken of but rarely achieved in a world that prioritizes speed, performance, and overload. However, finding and maintaining this balance is vital for our overall well-being. In this chapter, we will delve into the significance of balance in every aspect of life and explore practical tips for maintaining it on a mental, emotional, and physical level.

The Significance of Balance in All Life Aspects:

An Unbalanced Life Leads to Burn-out: Overexerting ourselves or neglecting certain areas of our life increases the risk of burn-out, stress, and exhaustion.

Inner Harmony: A balance in our lives often translates into inner peace, mental clarity, and a heightened ability to handle challenges.

Enhanced Relationships: When we are balanced, we tend to be more present and attentive to our loved ones, which can strengthen our bonds.

Tips to Maintain Mental, Emotional, and Physical Balance:

Define Your Priorities: Pinpoint what's crucial for you in life. This can help in balancing daily demands and focusing your energy where it's most needed.

Practice Emotional Regulation: Learn techniques, such as meditation or journaling, to process your emotions and maintain your emotional equilibrium.

Take Breaks: Whether it's a coffee break, a stroll in nature, or just a few deep breaths, taking short breaks can reset and balance your mind.

Regular Physical Activity: Movement, whether it's walking, yoga, or more intense exercises, can help balance both the body and mind.

Establish Boundaries: Learn to say no when required and set healthy limits to avoid being overwhelmed.

Balanced Nutrition: A nutritious and balanced diet can support your overall well-being, helping you feel at your best both physically and mentally.

Social Connection: Engaging with others, be it friends, family, or colleagues, can provide invaluable balance against isolation or work overload.

Conclusion:

Balance is not a final goal, but a continuous process that shapes our path to enduring happiness. It requires consistent reflection and adjustment, ensuring every aspect of our lives receives the attention it deserves. In cultivating balance, we not only find harmony in our daily routines but also foster a deeper sense of contentment and well-being. This equilibrium allows us to face life's challenges with poise and celebrate its joys with a grounded heart, leading us towards a more fulfilling and joyful existence.

Chapter 13: Inner Wisdom

Inner wisdom, that mysterious guide within each of us, is often overlooked amidst the chaos of modern life. Yet, it is one of the most profound and reliable sources of direction, understanding, and truth. In this chapter, we'll explore the art of connecting with this intuition, as well as methods to understand and listen to our own inner voice.

Connecting to One's Own Intuition:

Acknowledge the Presence of Intuition: Our intuition is that soft voice whispering advice, warnings, or encouragement. It often presents itself as a gut feeling or a "sense about something".

Make Room for Silence: In our noisy world, silence is crucial to hear our inner voice. Be it through meditation, walking in nature, or just granting oneself quiet moments, these pauses allow our intuition to surface.

Trust Your Feelings: Intuition isn't always logical. It operates on a deeper level than intellect. Learn to trust these instincts, even if they sometimes defy reason.

Understanding and Listening to Your Inner Voice:

Journaling: Keeping a diary is a great way to bring to light our inner thoughts. By writing regularly, we can start to discern patterns, desires, and concerns that might not be immediately apparent otherwise.

Contemplation: Pondering deep questions can help us better understand our inner voice. "What truly matters to me?", "How do I genuinely feel about this?" are examples of questions to explore.

Practice Active Listening: When we take the time to truly listen, without judgment or distraction, we can tap into a deeper understanding of our inner wisdom.

Look for Signs: Sometimes, our intuition shows itself through signs or synchronicities. Learn to recognize these moments and reflect upon them.

Conclusion:

Connecting to our inner wisdom is an ongoing journey. The more we trust, listen to, and act upon our intuition, the clearer and more guiding it becomes. This inner voice is an invaluable source of wisdom, inspiration, and truth that can illuminate our path towards happiness.

Journeying on the Road to Happiness:

The quest for happiness is universal, yet the paths we take to reach it are as varied as the stars in the sky. In this odyssey of life, certain elements prove to be true compasses for navigating towards a fulfilling existence.

At the heart of this quest, the connections we make with others often become our most treasured possessions. Deep, genuine relationships offer us moments of joy, support, and unconditional love. But just as a ship needs a destination, our lives gain depth when guided by a mission, a purpose propelling us forward.

However, life's winds don't always blow in the direction we hope for. That's when our adaptability becomes our greatest asset. It allows us to embrace life's changing waves with grace and resilience. And in this dance with life, kindness emerges as a soothing melody. By offering small acts of kindness, we illuminate our path and that of others.

The journey towards happiness is also an invitation to introspection and growth. It is through facing challenges and blossoming that we discover new facets of ourselves. And when the outside world becomes noisy, seeking solace in solitude provides a sanctuary, a chance to recharge.

But we must not underestimate the healing power of nature. Getting lost in its majesty, or simply surrounding ourselves with a calming environment, reconnects us to the very essence of life. And in these moments, what would life be without the lightness of laughter, the carefreeness of play, and the spontaneity of fun?

It's crucial to remember that happiness is not a destination but the journey itself. Each of us holds our own map, with its own landmarks. Thus, it's essential to listen to one's heart and adapt these guides to our own inner melody.

Conclusion

At the end of this journey through the 13 keys to happiness, it is essential to take a moment to reflect on what we've discovered and how we can integrate these lessons into our daily lives.

Gratitude reminds us to cherish and appreciate moments, big or small, that brighten our days.

Physical and Mental Health emphasizes the importance of taking care of our body and mind, the foundations of our well-being.

Healthy Relationships and Self-preservation teach us the balance between giving to others and taking time to rejuvenate ourselves.

With **Presence**, we learn to live in the current moment, away from distractions and worries.

Acceptance is the art of embracing life as it comes, with its ups and downs.

Connection highlights the importance of the bonds we forge with others and with the world around us.

Passion reminds us to embrace what drives us and gives meaning to our existence.

Resilience shows us that despite challenges, we have the strength to bounce back and persevere.

By practicing **Authenticity**, we remain true to ourselves and lead an authentic life.

Letting Go teaches us to release what we cannot control and to embrace life's flow.

With **Optimism**, we choose to see the light even in dark times.

Balance guides us in seeking harmony between the various aspects of our life.

Lastly, **Inner Wisdom** urges us to connect to that inner source of guidance and clarity.

These keys are not linear steps but interconnected pieces of a puzzle that, together, form the picture of happiness. Remember that happiness is a continuous journey, not a destination.

Thank you for accompanying me through these pages. May your quest for happiness be everlasting and fruitful.

As you close this book, remember that your pursuit of happiness is unique. Embrace each key at your own pace, integrate them into your life as you see fit. Continue to explore, learn, and above all, listen to your heart.

Don't wait for a future moment to be happy. Happiness is within reach, here and now. May your journey be filled with joy, discoveries, and unforgettable moments.

Continue to explore, learn, and grow. And most importantly, remember that happiness often lies in the little things, in the present moments, and in the sincerity with which we live each instant. Good luck in your quest for happiness!

Acknowledgments

Writing a book is a journey in itself, and this journey would not have been possible without the support, encouragement, and contributions of many individuals.

First and foremost, thank you to my loved ones for their unwavering support, wise advice, and infinite patience.

I also wish to express my gratitude to all the experts, authors, and thinkers whose work inspired and guided me throughout the writing of this book.

To all my readers, thank you for granting me your time and trust. Your quest for happiness is a source of inspiration for me, and I am honored to be a part of your journey.

Lastly, I'd like to thank the members of the editorial team for their expertise, passion, and dedication in making this book a reality.

Every person mentioned, and so many others not mentioned, have played an essential role in the creation of this work. Thank you from the bottom of my heart ♥.

Tom Levy

Appendices

Additional Resources:

In this section, you will find a selection of online resources, workshops, conferences, and tools to help deepen your understanding of each key and continue your journey towards happiness.

Guided Meditation:

• **Headspace:** A website and mobile app offering guided meditation sessions for all levels.
• **Calm:** Also offers meditations, bedtime stories, and breathing techniques.

Gratitude Journals:
   • **The Five Minute Journal:** A structured journal to help you start and end each day with gratitude.
   • **Good Days Start With Gratitude:** A 52-week gratitude journal to cultivate an attitude of gratitude.

List of Podcasts:
   • **"The Happiness Lab" by Dr. Laurie Santos:** Explores the latest scientific research on happiness.
   • **"Ten Percent Happier" with Dan Harris:** Explores how meditation can make life better.

Mobile Apps:
• **Day One:** A journaling app that can be used to note moments of gratitude.
• **Smiling Mind:** A meditation and well-being app that offers programs tailored for all ages.

It should be noted that full access to some apps or platforms may require a payment, but many offer free content to allow users to start their journey.

These resources are widely recognized and have been praised for their effectiveness and accessibility. However, it's always a good idea to do your own research and see which resource resonates most with you personally.

Bibliography

Below is a list of books that have inspired or complemented the content of this work. These readings are ideal for those who wish to continue their pursuit of happiness.

1. **"The Art of Meditation"** by Matthieu Ricard: This French Buddhist monk provides a clear approach to meditation and its importance in the pursuit of happiness.
2. **"The Power of Joy"** by Frédéric Lenoir: In this work, the philosopher and writer explores the nature of joy and suggests ways to attain it.
3. **"The Miracle of Mindfulness"** by Thich Nhat Hanh: Although the author is not French, this book has had a significant impact in France. It offers an introduction to the practice of mindfulness.
4. **"Three Friends in Search of Wisdom"** by Christophe André, Alexandre Jollien, and Matthieu Ricard: Three contemporary thinkers share their reflections on life, happiness, and wisdom.
5. **"Happy Like a Dane"** by Malene Rydahl: While the main subject is happiness in Denmark, the author, of Danish origin but living in France, provides a unique perspective on what constitutes happiness across cultures.

6. **"The Power of Now"** by Eckhart Tolle: In this transformative spiritual guide, Tolle delves into the concept of the "now" as the key to ending mental suffering. He encourages us to transcend our time-based ego to reach a higher state of consciousness, where peace is attained by living fully in the present.

7. **"The Happiness Project"** by Gretchen Rubin: Rubin, in a quest to improve her everyday life, gives herself a year to increase her happiness. Each month, she sets resolutions and challenges, offering readers practical insights and tips for finding more joy in life's small moments.

8. **"The Art of Happiness"** by the Dalai Lama: Through interviews with psychiatrist Howard Cutler, the Dalai Lama shares his views on how to lead a happy and fulfilling life. He explores the nature of happiness and suggests ways to overcome barriers to joy, emphasizing compassion and meditation.

9. **"Authentic Happiness"** by Martin E. P. Seligman: Seligman, the founder of positive psychology, presents his theory that happiness can be cultivated by identifying and using our unique strengths and virtues. He provides tools and questionnaires to help readers discover their own sources of genuine happiness.

10. **"The Gifts of Imperfection"** by Brené Brown: Brené Brown, a social science

researcher, delves into how embracing our imperfections can lead to living a more courageous, compassionate, and authentic life. She encourages readers to shed what they "should" be to celebrate who they truly are.

11. **"Flow: The Psychology of Optimal Experience"** by Mihaly Csikszentmihalyi.